GODS OF OLYMPUS

 W9-BAF-951

LEVEL **3** READER

READING LEVEL — GRADES 2 TO 4

Written by Kathryn Knight
Illustrated by Ezra Tucker
Medusa by Michelangelo Merisi da Caravaggio, circa 1597

The Olympians

Long ago—in the days of myth and legend—Uranus (**Yer**-ah-nuhs) was Father Sky. His wife was Gaia (**Gye**-uh), Mother Earth. From them came giant beings, called Titans, who lived on Earth. Cronus (**Crow**-nuhs), a Titan, was the father of many powerful gods. His son Zeus (**Zuce**) became king of all the gods who ruled during the old days of Greece.

Most of the gods lived on Mount Olympus, the highest mountain in Greece. They were called the Twelve Olympians.

When Zeus called the Olympians together,
they formed the pantheon
(Greek word meaning "of all gods").

Zeus

Zeus was the king of the gods and master of the universe. You could hear his voice in the mighty roar of thunder. His bolts of lightning reminded all the gods and the people of Earth that he was in charge.

Zeus had a golden throne on Mount Olympus, but he liked to go down to Earth and meddle in the lives of people. His sister Hera served as his queen. He was a strong but fair ruler of mankind and the gods. He was quick to laugh, but he was also quick to punish any liar or law-breaker. When he was in a joyful mood, the Earth enjoyed days of sunshine. When he was angry, fierce storms raged through the sky.

ZEUS
TITLES: King of the Gods; Lord of the Sky; God of Rain
BORN TO: Cronus and Rhea
SYMBOL: Lightning Bolt
SACRED ANIMAL: Eagle
ROMAN NAME: Jupiter

Like the ancient Greeks, the Romans also worshipped gods, but they had different names for them. The Roman king of the gods was called Jupiter.

Hera

Hera (**Here**-uh) was a goddess, a female god. She was the queen of the gods and all mankind. The other Olympians respected her, and some were more loyal to her than to her brother Zeus. She cared greatly for her own beauty and wore fine makeup and perfumes. It was said that her lotion filled the universe with a lovely fragrance.

Hera was much more serious than Zeus. In fact, she did not approve of his playful ways and often argued with him. If Zeus thought another goddess or human was more beautiful than Hera, she became jealous. The other Olympians tried to stay out of her way when her jealous temper was on the loose!

HERA
TITLES: Queen of the Gods; Goddess of Marriage and Family
BORN TO: Cronus and Rhea
SYMBOL: Pomegranate
SACRED ANIMALS: Cow; Peacock
ROMAN NAME: Juno

Hera's loyal watchman was Argus who had 100 eyes.
When he was killed, Hera honored him
by preserving his eyes in the tail of a peacock.

Poseidon

Zeus made his brother Poseidon (Poe-**sye**-den) god of the seas. Poseidon had a throne on Mount Olympus, but he preferred his jeweled palace beneath the waves.

Humans had great respect for this moody, bad-tempered god. They needed his help and dreaded his anger. He could blow fair winds into the sails of ships. He could also still the winds so that no ship could sail. One flick of his powerful trident could shake the ground and send a *tsunami* (huge ocean wave) crashing to the shore, swallowing an entire coastal town.

Poseidon's son was a Cyclops, a one-eyed giant, named Polyphemus (Polly-**fee**-muss). When the hero Odysseus (Oh-**diss**-ee-uhs) blinded Polyphemus, Poseidon took revenge! He sent violent waves and winds that blew Odysseus's ship completely off course.

Though he ruled the seas,
it was Poseidon who breathed
life into the first horse.

POSEIDON

TITLES: GOD OF THE SEAS;
GOD OF HORSES; EARTH-SHAKER
BORN TO: CRONUS AND RHEA
SYMBOL: TRIDENT (A FORKED STAFF)
SACRED ANIMALS: DOLPHIN; HORSE
ROMAN NAME: NEPTUNE

Athena

Of all of Zeus's children, his favorite was Athena (Uh-**theen**-uh), a wise, bold goddess who sprang fully formed— wearing armor!— from Zeus's head. Athena became very involved in the lives of

The Parthenon, the temple of Athena, was built on the Acropolis, the highest ground of Athens.

humans. She taught them the skills of weaving, sewing, farming and metalworking. In this way, Athena was the Olympian who helped humans to settle into communities and become civilized.

Athena was the goddess of war. However, she was more an advisor and protector than a fighter, encouraging strategy and justice. She helped the Greeks triumph over enemies, and they named their largest city, Athens, after her.

ATHENA
TITLES: GODDESS OF WISDOM;
GODDESS OF WAR AND MILITARY ARTS
BORN TO: ZEUS
(OUT FROM THE TOP OF HIS HEAD)
SYMBOLS: SPINNER'S DISTAFF;
AEGIS (SHIELD)
SACRED ANIMAL: OWL
ROMAN NAME: MINERVA

Athena carried an aegis (shield) that struck fear into the enemy. It bore the head of Medusa, a female monster with hair of snakes. If anyone looked upon the face of Medusa, he would turn to stone!

Ares

Ares (**Air**-eez) was the half-brother of Athena. Like his sister, he was a god of war. Unlike his wise, skillful sister, Ares was bloodthirsty and vengeful. He cared little for the art and skill of battle. Ares was the spirit of all that was cruel and violent in war. Anytime arguments arose between people or nations, Ares drove his chariot into the action, stirring up a battle, not caring who won or lost.

ARES
TITLE: GOD OF WAR
BORN TO: ZEUS AND HERA
SYMBOLS: BRONZE SPEAR;
FIGHTING DOGS
SACRED ANIMALS:
SERPENT; VULTURE
ROMAN NAME: MARS

Ares placed the Drakon—a dragon-like serpent—
in a cave to guard Ares's spring of magical waters.
Cadmus, a young warrior, slew the Drakon,
and Athena told Cadmus to plant the teeth of the
monster. From the ground sprang fully armored
soldiers called the Spartoi.

Ares was tall and handsome, but conceited and uncaring.
He was disliked by most of the Olympians. There was one
goddess, however, who loved him. It was Aphrodite, the
goddess of love—proving that opposites do attract!

Apollo

Apollo (Uh-**paul**-oh) was a noble god, representing light, truth, healing, and the arts. He was handsome, young, and intelligent. He played music on the lyre and lute and won music contests with other gods. Apollo had the gift of prophecy, and the Greeks prayed to him for answers about the future. As the god of medicine, he could bring sickness yet also cure disease.

APOLLO

TITLES: GOD OF LIGHT; GOD OF MUSIC AND POETRY; GOD OF PROPHECY AND TRUTH; GOD OF MEDICINE

BORN TO: ZEUS AND LETO, A TITAN

SYMBOLS: LYRE; LAUREL TREE; BOW AND ARROW

SACRED ANIMALS: WOLF; SWAN; RAVEN; CICADA; DOLPHIN

ROMAN NAME: APOLLO

Artemis

Apollo's twin sister was Artemis (**Ar**-teh-miss), the protector of nature and wild animals, especially the young. However, she was also a skilled hunter, riding through the sky at night with arrows of silver moonlight. Like Apollo, Artemis was a friend to humans. She watched over women during childbirth and guarded young girls.

ARTEMIS

TITLES: GODDESS OF THE HUNT AND WILD ANIMALS; GODDESS OF THE MOON
BORN TO: ZEUS AND LETO, A TITAN
SYMBOLS: GOLDEN BOW AND ARROWS
SACRED ANIMALS: DEER; SNAKE; BOAR
ROMAN NAME: DIANA

Demeter was protector of the growth and life of vegetation. She taught humans how to farm the land and introduced them to wheat. This allowed humans to live easier, more peaceful lives.

Demeter

Demeter (Deh-**mee**-ter), the harvest goddess, had a daughter named Persephone (Per-**seff**-oh-nee) who caught the eye of Pluto, god of the underworld.

He took Persephone to his dark, gloomy regions below, leaving Demeter in despair. During Demeter's sad search for her lost daughter, a hard cold settled over the earth, killing grains and flowers. Zeus ordered Pluto to send Persephone back, and Demeter was overjoyed. Her tears of joy watered the earth, the sun shone, and plants once more began to grow. But her joy was short-lived. Persephone had to return and live with Pluto four months of every year. And so, during these four months, Demeter's grief brings Winter. Upon her daughter's return, Demeter's joy brings Spring, reawakening the earth.

DEMETER

TITLES: Goddess of the Harvest; Goddess of Agriculture; Bringer of Seasons

BORN TO: Cronus and Rhea

SYMBOLS: Ear of Wheat; Grains; Poppy; Cornucopia

SACRED ANIMALS: Pig; Dove; Snake

ROMAN NAME: Ceres

Aphrodite

The most beautiful Olympian was Aphrodite (Aff-row-**dye**-tee), the goddess of love. She enjoyed admiration and often peered into her hand mirror to review her makeup and perfectly curled lashes. Queen Hera was jealous of Aphrodite's youth and loveliness, but there was no denying that the goddess of love was the fairest of all.

One look from Aphrodite could make any man fall in love with her. And she certainly delighted in winning hearts. But her own heart

APHRODITE
TITLES: Goddess of Love and Beauty; Goddess of Joy
BORN TO: Uranus and the foam on the sea
SYMBOLS: Mirror; seashell; cupid; apple
SACRED ANIMALS: Dove; sparrow; swan; hare
ROMAN NAME: Venus

belonged to Ares, the god of war. Their child—
a mix of love and war—was Harmonia, goddess
of harmony. Another of Aphrodite's children
was Eros, the winged cupid who accompanied
her everywhere with his bow and arrows of love.

Prince Paris was asked to name "the fairest" goddess.
Hera bribed him with promises of power. Athena offered
glory in battle. But he chose Aphrodite, who promised
him the love of the most beautiful woman.

Hephaestus

Hera was disappointed in her son Hephaestus (Heh-**fess**-tus) because he was lame and ugly. Yet this kind, lovable god proved to be talented and valuable. He became a master craftsman, building palaces and making armor for the Olympians. In his blacksmith workshop deep within the volcano Mt. Aetna, Hephaestus created Zeus's lightning bolts.

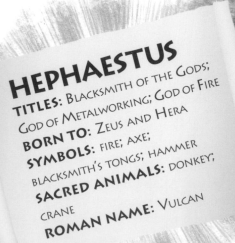

HEPHAESTUS

TITLES: BLACKSMITH OF THE GODS; GOD OF METALWORKING; GOD OF FIRE

BORN TO: ZEUS AND HERA

SYMBOLS: FIRE; AXE; BLACKSMITH'S TONGS; HAMMER

SACRED ANIMALS: DONKEY; CRANE

ROMAN NAME: VULCAN

Hermes

Only one Olympian was permitted to go to all parts of the world: Olympus, earth, *and* the underworld. This was Hermes (**Her**-meez), beloved son and helper of Zeus. This swift-footed god served as the gods' messenger as well as the guide for human souls to the underworld after death.

HERMES

TITLES: MESSENGER OF THE GODS; GUIDE OF THE DEAD; GOD OF TRAVEL

BORN TO: ZEUS AND MAIA, A MOUNTAIN NYMPH

SYMBOL: CADUCEUS (WINGED STAFF ENTWINED WITH SNAKES)

SACRED ANIMALS: HAWK; TORTOISE; RAM

ROMAN NAME: MERCURY

Dionysus believed in a "don't worry, be happy"
approach to life. He was happy to help anyone in
need. He was playful and full of laughter. And he
encouraged the arts of playwriting and acting.

Dionysus

One of the most popular Olympians was Dionysus (Dye-oh-**nye**-sus), the lighthearted god of wine and festivities. This handsome young god liked to hang out on earth, partying and traveling.

Dionysus had not always been an Olympian. At one time, Hestia (**Hess**-tee-ah), the goddess of home and family, held a place on Olympus. She was the most tender, loving, and forgiving goddess. Her heart's desire was to tend the earthly home-fires and protect orphans and missing children. She chose to give up her place on Olympus to serve the humans she loved. And who inherited her special spot on Olympus? Dionysus—who spent most of his time partying on earth!

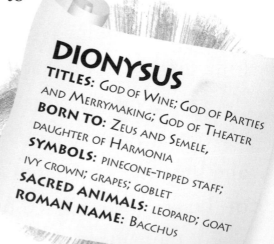

DIONYSUS

TITLES: God of Wine; God of Parties and Merrymaking; God of Theater

BORN TO: Zeus and Semele, daughter of Harmonia

SYMBOLS: pinecone-tipped staff; ivy crown; grapes; goblet

SACRED ANIMALS: leopard; goat

ROMAN NAME: Bacchus

The Height of the Gods

The Olympians shared the ancient world with lesser gods, half-gods, monsters, and magical beings. These filled Greek myths with tales of humor, horror, and wonder—such as the story of Pegasus, the winged horse.

Pegasus was born to Poseidon and the monstrous, snake-haired Medusa. The horse refused to be tamed, but one hero captured him, using a golden bridle from Athena. When the young man tried to ride Pegasus to Mount Olympus, Zeus sent a fly to sting the horse—and the hero who dared to reach for the height of the gods was tossed back to earth.

For there can only be Twelve Olympians.